King Arthur Needs You!

Chris Baker

Illustrated by Yannick Robert

OXFORD
UNIVERSITY PRESS

New adventurers start here!

This book asks *you* to choose what happens next. To discover how your choices work out, you turn to the page numbers given on the signposts. When you reach the end, why not start again? If you make different choices, you can have a whole new adventure.

Start

Welcome to my castle. I am King Arthur. I wonder why you've come to see me. Do you want to become a Knight of the Round Table? You'll need to go and have an adventure and then come back to tell me what you've done. If your adventure makes you a worthy Knight, you can join us.

Or do you want to become the apprentice of my wizard, Merlin? He's the greatest wizard ever, but learning magic can be difficult and dangerous. In fact, they say that one of Merlin's last apprentices got turned into an armchair by accident – so be careful! Tell me, what do you want to do?

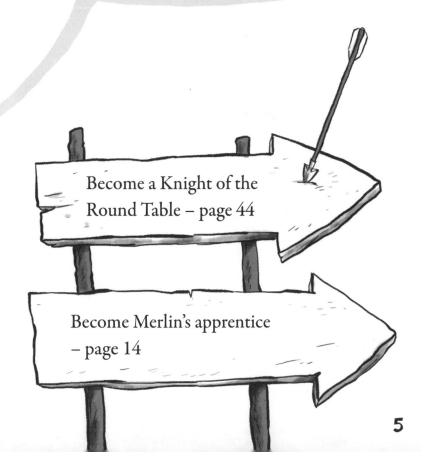

Become a Knight of the Round Table – page 44

Become Merlin's apprentice – page 14

Join in the siege of Sir Foulplay's castle

Sir Foulplay isn't going to come out of his castle and you can see how difficult it is going to be to get in – unless Sir Foulplay's drawbridge can be lowered.

'I can think of two plans,' you say. 'Do you see that lever which makes the drawbridge come down? Well, I have a magic football. My first plan is to kick the football so that it knocks the lever. When the drawbridge comes down, we can rush in and capture Sir Foulplay and his gang. But it's a very difficult kick, and I might miss.

My second plan is to challenge Sir Foulplay
and his gang to a game of football. If he wins,
we'll all go away. If he loses the match, he and
his gang must surrender.'

Which plan will you try?

Take a penalty kick to open
the drawbridge – page 50

Play in a football match
– page 38

Save the villagers from the giant kidnapper

You go to the village which is bothered by a giant, and find him easily.

He's chasing a little boy. The giant has an enormous club made out of an uprooted tree. He has decorated it with daisy chains, but it still looks very fearsome.

'Leave that boy alone!' you shout.

'Oh, goody,' calls the giant. 'Playtime!' And he comes rushing towards you. What do you do?

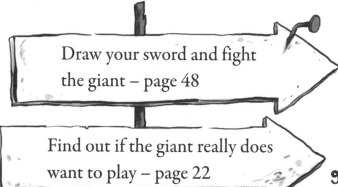

Draw your sword and fight the giant – page 48

Find out if the giant really does want to play – page 22

Choose the jar with the square

You bring the Lady of the Lake some tea made from the jar with the square. She seems to be telling the armchair a joke.

'Ah, thank you,' she says, taking the tea. 'It smells delicious.'

When she drinks the tea, something very odd indeed happens – the Lady of the Lake completely vanishes!

'Oh, I see,' says a voice from where she was sitting a moment ago. 'You seem to have made me a cup of Invisibili-tea. But I expect Merlin keeps an antidote on the same shelf where you found this tea. Go back and make me a different tea so that I can be visible again.'

So you go back to the tea shelf. The jar with the circle is still there. There's also a jar with a triangle. One of those two jars must be the antidote!

Which one do you try this time?

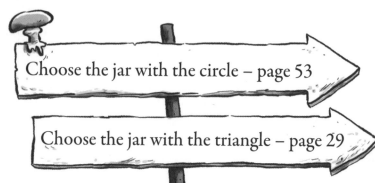

Choose the jar with the circle – page 53

Choose the jar with the triangle – page 29

Choose the magic football

You set off with the football. After a while you meet Sir Lancelot, the bravest of King Arthur's knights (and the unbeatable card in King Arthur's Knights trump cards).

'We could do with some help,' says Sir Lancelot. 'Sir Foulplay the False, the evil leader of a gang of robber knights, is hiding in his castle and he won't come out. We can't work out how to defeat him. But we also need someone to go and help the villagers deal with a giant who has been trying to catch their children.'

Which adventure do you choose?

SIR LANCELOT

KING ARTHUR'S BEST KNIGHT

SPECIAL POWER	100%
INTELLIGENCE	100%
STRENGTH	100%
	100%

Join in the siege of Sir Foulplay's castle – page 6

Save the villagers from the giant kidnapper – page 9

Become Merlin's apprentice

'Welcome, child,' says Merlin the wizard when you get to his tower. People say he's a thousand years old, but he's full of energy and cleverness. He also seems to be in a terrible hurry.

'I'd like to give you a proper magic lesson right away, but I really must go and see the King immediately about something urgent. Can you wait here? I'm expecting a visitor shortly. If she comes before I am back, can you make tea for her?'

And off he strides down the stairs.

You look around Merlin's tower. What a mess! Merlin has a huge stuffed dragon, lots of pots of bubbling and smoking liquid, several weird-looking machines, and maps and books everywhere. He also *really* needs to tidy up the used pizza delivery boxes.

You're sure a huge book is growling at you. It's a good thing it's fixed to the wall with a strong chain.

There are two ravens on a perch.

They both laugh with a nasty croaking sound.

Just as it's getting a bit creepy, a voice calls up from below.

'Hello! Merlin! Are you there?'

You go to see who the visitor is.

It's the Lady of the Lake, the famous magician, magic weapon-maker, and judge of the magic talent competition, The Hex Factor. You explain that this is your first day as Merlin's new apprentice, that Merlin will be back soon, and that you've been asked to look after visitors.

'Not to worry,' says the Lady, kindly. 'Did you know I used to be Merlin's apprentice once too? If it's your first day you probably haven't found the sitting room yet. I'll show you where it is, and then you can make me some tea.'

The Lady of the Lake leads you to the sitting room and settles down in an armchair. You can't help but notice that she says –

Hello, Trevor!

– to the armchair before sitting down, but you don't have time to ask any questions. You go looking for the tea.

You find a shelf that has several jars on it. The shelf is labelled, but something messy is smeared over the labels, so you can only read the end bits. The jars also have messy labels, and it's not clear what most of them are, but two of them definitely say something-tea (you can just read the 'tea' bit). One jar has a circle painted on it, the other has a square.

Which jar will you use to make tea for the Lady of the Lake?

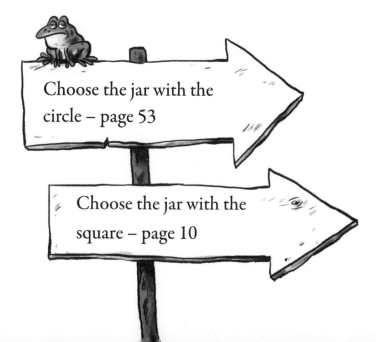

Choose the jar with the circle – page 53

Choose the jar with the square – page 10

Choose the Grungy Mop of Camelot

You set off, carrying your mop.

Before long you come to a village. The Mayor rushes up to you.

'Thank goodness that King Arthur has sent someone!' he says. 'A dragon is living in the cave up there and we're afraid it's going to attack us. We can't stand its awful roaring any longer! It goes on all day and all night. Please do something!'

He gives you a rope, and you climb up to the cave. The roaring is really loud, and you can smell a nasty rotten stench. Now you have to decide what to do next.

ROOᵒARR

Talk to the dragon – page 40

Draw your sword and rush into the dragon's cave – page 26

Find out if the giant really does want to play

The giant looks at you hopefully.

'OK, I'll play with you,' you say. 'Look, I've got a football!'

All afternoon, you and the giant have the best game of football ever. The magic football goes wherever the kicker wants it to, so the two of you can do some amazing shots.

'You're so much more fun to play with than those children,' says the giant. 'I didn't hurt any of them, but they all got scared and ran away.'

'If we can get the children safely back home, I think I can help both you and the villagers,' you say.

When you find the children, you convince them that the giant only wanted to play. You bring all the children back safe and sound, and the villagers are delighted.

'The giant isn't evil, but he *is* lonely, and he doesn't understand people very well,' you tell the villagers. 'So he thought he could make friends by forcing people to do what he wants. It was just a mistake. All he really wants to do is to play.'

So the villagers agree to be friends with the giant. With his great strength he is very useful helping on their farms, and the children play football with him every evening.

The villagers are so grateful that the Mayor rides back to King Arthur's castle with you, to tell King Arthur that you certainly should be made a Knight of the Round Table.

The End!   or   Try another adventure! Return to the start on page 4.

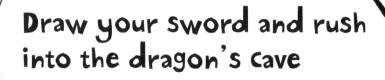

Draw your sword and rush into the dragon's cave

With a brave yell you rush in to fight the dragon.

This is not a good idea. The Dragon has black belts in kick-boxing, flame-throwing, knight-stomping, ninja sword-fighting and muffin decorating.

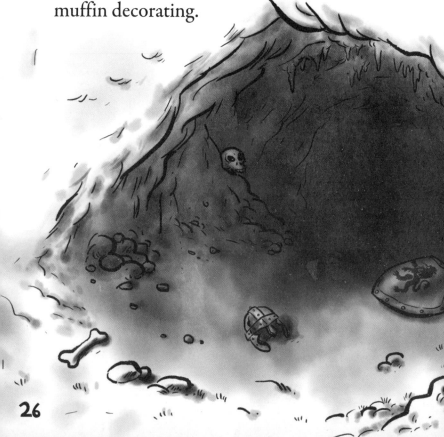

The world record for climbing-down-a-rope-while-your-pants-are-on-fire is 10.3 seconds. You do it in 9.8 seconds. Then you jump into a pond to extinguish your smouldering underwear.

At the foot of the cliff, who should you see but Sir Lancelot, one of King Arthur's most famous knights. Your teenage sister has cheesy posters of him all over her bedroom, but he's secretly your hero too.

'Don't let this get you down!' says Sir Lancelot, helping you out of the pond. 'True knights never give up. Often, fighting is not the way to get what you want. Go back and try talking to the dragon.'

Talk to the dragon
– page 40

Choose the jar with the triangle

You bring the Lady of the Lake some tea made from the jar with the triangle.

'Well, let's find out what this one does,' says the Lady of the Lake. 'You might want to stand back, just in case it's Hyperactivi-tea or even Tea-n-tea!'

'Just hope it isn't Calami-tea!' says another voice. It really seems to come from the armchair, but that's impossible ... isn't it?

The Lady of the Lake drinks the tea, while you watch anxiously.

With an odd sort of sparkle effect, she turns back into her usual self.

'Yes, that was definitely Normali-tea,' she says. 'I feel quite back to normal. I could still do with a cup of English breakfast tea, but maybe we should stop here!'

Just then Merlin arrives.

'What's this?' he thunders. 'You've been giving potions to my guests?'

You're getting worried that you'll get the sack, when you realize that both Merlin and the Lady of the Lake are laughing.

'Merlin, you're the most terrible trickster,' she says. 'It's a wonder that anyone manages to cope with you at all!'

'Not at all, my dear,' says Merlin. 'Magic is a dangerous thing. I must have an apprentice who understands that, who does as they are told and doesn't panic if unexpected things happen. So this was a serious test for my new assistant,' he says, looking at you and smiling, 'though I must admit I do like to have some fun as well.'

'It *was* funny when I had all those teas', says the Lady of the Lake. 'Merlin, do you remember *my* first day? I gave Sir Kay some Croak-a-Cola and turned him into a frog. Then I got the bottle of Demon-ade instead of the antidote!'

You watch them happily remembering how the Lady of the Lake accidently turned Sir Kay into a demon.

'Master,' you say, 'is being your apprentice often like this?'

'Oh, no,' says Merlin. 'Sometimes it's *much* weirder. One of my apprentices blew up my whole tower on her second day!'

He looks meaningfully at the Lady of the Lake.

'Tea-n-tea instead of English breakfast tea –
a simple mistake anyone could have made!'
says the Lady, pretending to be offended.
Then she giggles. 'The tower caught fire and
a flaming stuffed dragon went right through
the Queen's window and landed in her bath!
She was running around in her bathrobe,
shouting that monsters were attacking the
castle! All the knights came running and one
of them fell in the bath with his armour on!'

There's something you just have to ask.

'But is it true that one of your apprentices turned himself into an armchair and couldn't be turned back?'

Hah!

– says a voice, and this time you're really sure that it *is* the armchair talking.

'People always get that the wrong way around,' says the chair. 'I started as Merlin's armchair and he turned me into an apprentice when a few of you humans had been no good at it. Being an apprentice was fun for a while, but it just wasn't the same. If you're a human and you ask people to sit on you, they just think you're odd. So in the end I decided to go back to what I like best.'

Trevor gives a contented sigh.

'So, child,' says Merlin. 'You've done well. What do you think? It's not too late to change your mind about being my apprentice, if you don't want to work with a crazy old man.'

You look around Merlin's amazing cluttered home, past his talking armchair and at the kindly smiling face of Merlin himself.

'Master,' you say, 'I want to be your apprentice more than anything in the world.'

The End!   or   Try another adventure! Return to the start on page 4.

Play in a football match

Sir Foulplay thinks it is a great idea to decide the battle by having a football match. He's not particularly good at football, but he *is* extremely good at cheating.

Sir Foulplay won't let you use your magic football for the game in case it helps you to win. He wants to use Sir Lancelot's teddy bear mascot as the football instead.
When Sir Lancelot refuses, Sir Foulplay sulks. While Sir Lancelot is distracted, all of Sir Foulplay's gang draw their swords and attack Sir Lancelot's army.

However, because Sir Foulplay *always* cheats, Sir Lancelot's army are ready for the battle. Soon, Sir Foulplay and his gang realize they're beaten, and run back into their castle. You're back to square one.

'Nice try, but it didn't work,' says Sir Lancelot.

Take a penalty kick to open the drawbridge – page 50

Save the villagers from the giant kidnapper – page 9

Talk to the dragon

'Hello, dragon!' you shout. 'I've just come to ask whether you can be quieter, please? You're frightening the villagers!'

The dragon's roars turn into sobs.

'I can't help it,' says the dragon. 'I have such a toothache.'

Then you have a great idea.

'If you let me come into the cave and open your mouth, I'll try to help,' you say.

The dragon's cave is dark and smelly, and you can just about see the huge dragon crouched inside. The dragon has revolting stinky breath, but you climb right inside its mouth.

'Well, no wonder you have toothache,' you say. 'You can't have cleaned your teeth for *ages*. Lots of bits of rotten ogre are stuck between them. Stay still and I'll clean you up.'

It is a long and disgusting job, using the mop as a toothbrush and the rope as dental floss. Only a brave knight could do it.

When you've finished, the mop has given the dragon's teeth a magical minty gleam, and the dragon is delighted.

'I feel so much better!' it says. But then it looks sad once more. 'The trouble is, I can't clean my own teeth, so they will just get dirty and sore again.'

'Come with me to King Arthur's castle,' you say. 'Someone will clean your teeth every day, and in return you can help King Arthur with his battles.'

When you fly back to the castle on a dragon, King Arthur is so impressed that he makes you a Knight of the Round Table right there and then!

The End! or Try another adventure! Return to the start on page 4.

Become a Knight of the Round Table

King Arthur has told you that a good way to start your adventure would be to go and see the Lady of the Lake, a powerful magician who can give you a magic item.

So here you are at the Lake. You call the Lady, but a boy's voice says, 'What do you want?'

'Er ... you're not the Lady of the Lake,' you say.

After a while, a teenage boy rises up out of the water carrying two items.

'Here you are,' says the Lad of the Lake. 'You're lucky, we've got a choice of very powerful magic items. Which one do you want?'

'Um, I *was* hoping for a magic sword or a helmet ... ' you say.

'There aren't any left!' says the Lad of the Lake. 'It's the Grungy Mop of Camelot, or a football made in the magic workshop of the FA – the Fairies' Association! Anyway, that's what we've got, so choose one quick – I'm watching TV. Er ... I mean I'm busy using talking furniture to see events far away! You don't want to interrupt that kind of sorcery!'

So, if you're forced to choose between a mop and a magic football, what do you pick?

Choose the Grungy Mop of Camelot – page 20

Choose the magic football – page 13

Draw your sword and fight the giant

With a superhuman whack of his club, the giant squashes you flat and then stomps off to find someone else to play with.

There you are, stuck inside your flattened armour, like a tin can that has been run over by a car. After a while, the Lady of the Lake comes along.

'Oh dear,' she says. 'Another knight who tried to fight the giant.' She gets out her magic bicycle pump and pumps you back up to your normal shape.

'It's no good trying to fight the giant,' says the Lady of the Lake. 'Find him again and see if he really does just want someone to play with.'

Find out if the giant really does want to play – page 22

Take a penalty kick to open the drawbridge

You aim carefully at the drawbridge lever. But just as you kick, you notice the castle laundry flapping in the wind. Unfortunately, one of the football's magical powers is that it goes wherever the kicker is looking. With an amazing swerve, the ball whizzes past the lever and right through the line of laundry. Wrapped in a pair of Sir Foulplay's underpants, the ball shoots like a comet across the castle, hitting the cook on the head. She falls head first into the porridge she's making.

The ball's other magical power is that it always finds a way to get back to its owner.

'Must ... take ... ball ... back,' says Cook, letting down the drawbridge. 'Must ... return ... ball ... then ... finish ... making ... underpants ... porridge.'

Sir Lancelot and his army rush past Cook into the castle, and in no time at all Sir Foulplay and his gang have surrendered.

'Well done, Sir Knight,' Sir Lancelot says to you at the victory feast. 'I'm sure King Arthur will make you a Knight of the Round Table now. By the way, this porridge is lovely. A most unusual flavour. I can't think why you won't have any.'

The End!

or

Try another adventure! Return to the start on page 4.

Choose the jar with the circle

You make tea from the jar with the circle and take it to the Lady of the Lake. It seems she is having a conversation with the armchair, but you can't be quite sure.

'Ah, thank you, child,' she says, and drinks the tea.

To your horror, she starts to change. Her arms, legs and body become huge, hairy and muscly. Her head becomes enormous and warty, with gigantic tusks and horns. She sprouts a scaly tail with spikes on the end like a dinosaur. She has turned into a monster!

'Ah,' says the Lady of the Lake, surprisingly calmly for someone who is now breathing out green smoke. 'I think you must have made me a cup of Monstrosi-tea by mistake. Not to worry. Merlin's bound to have an antidote. It's probably another kind of tea. Go and find it and make me another cup of tea that will put things right.'

You rush back to the tea shelf. The jars with the circle and square are still there. There's also a jar with a triangle.

Which one do you try this time?

Choose the jar with the square – page 10

Choose the jar with the triangle – page 29

About the author

When I was a kid I was given a book a bit like this. It was a pirate story and I enjoyed it a lot, but there was only one way to get through the story without being eaten by a giant squid or coming to some other nasty end. I remember getting frustrated about that! So I decided that nobody would get killed or lost forever in this story – I made it so that if you did make a "wrong" choice, something funny would happen to you and then you would get a chance to try again.